<u>Demonology and Deliverance</u>

Understanding Demonic Operations

By

David Okumgba

ISBN: 1-4107-0062-3 (e-book)
ISBN: 1-4107-0063-1 (Paperback)

Library of Congress Control Number: 2002096325

This book is printed on acid free paper.

Printed in the United States of America
Bloomington, IN

1stBooks - rev. 01/03/03

Unless otherwise stated, all scriptural quotations are from the *King James Version, New King James Version* and the *New International Version* of the Bible.

In some of the testimonies the real names of the testifiers were not used in other to protect their identity.

David Okumgba
P. O. Box 1395
Alief, Texas 77411
E-mail; okumgbadavid@hotmail.com

DEDICATION

'Beloved Holy Spirit, My Counselor, My Comforter, My teacher and Mentor I dedicate this book unto you in the name of Jesus Christ. This book is also dedicated to my lovely wife, Margaret and to the graduating class of 2001, Power Bible Institute.

CONTENTS

INTRODUCTION

The greatest weapon of the devil is ignorance. Hosea 4:6 says *'my people perish for lack of knowledge'*. History is replete with stories of lives, careers, marriages, families, and whole tribes, cities and even nations that have been destroyed for lack of knowledge. Even now many people, particularly Christian homes, lives and churches are being destroyed because they are ignorant of the devices of the enemy. Apostle Paul said in 2 Corinthians 2:11 that we should not be ignorant of the devices of the devil lest the devil takes advantage of us. How can we overcome if we do not understand the strategies, techniques and tricks of the enemy. An important element of successful warfare even in the secular world is knowing your enemy, his strengths and weaknesses. That is why governments spend huge sums of money on espionage. In fact you are as strong as the weakness of your enemy.

The reason why the devil seems to be running circles around believers is because the church is yet to assume her proper authority vis-à-vis the powers of darkness. And the church was not able to assume her proper authority because she is ignorant of the devices of the devil. She does not have a correct assessment of her adversary. Every trick of the devil comes as a shock and surprise and most often the church does not know how to respond. We fight as if beating the air. For a long time the church taught that the devil has no power. Some even taught that there is no devil or at best they reduce the devil to an inanimate euphemism called negativity. But if the devil has no power than he would not be a worthy opponent of God. Because the strength of your opponent is an indication of your own strength. Even the scriptures recognize that the devil has some power. Luke 10:19 says we have been given power above the POWER OF THE DEVIL. Ezekiel 28:14 calls the devil the ANOINTED CHERUB. And to the best of my knowledge that anointing has not been taken away from him. In the end times according to Revelation 11 through 14 the devil will use that anointing to perform signs and lying wonders such that he will even call fire down from heaven in the sight of every one. The devil is still anointed. We must not take him for granted.

Do not be shocked, I am not trying to glorify the devil. I am trying to make you see that the devil is a threat we should not be ignorant of. We ought to deliberately prepare our minds for his assault and through the Holy Ghost devise battle strategies to frustrate his devices. Nevertheless He that is in us is greater than he that is in the world. We have power and authority over all the powers of the enemy. Compared to God and to us the devil is powerless.

Jesus said in John 8:32; '*and you shall know the truth and the truth shall make you free*. Proverbs 4:7 says '*wisdom is the principal thing; therefore get wisdom. And in all your getting, get understanding.* This book is an attempt to make knowledge of the operations of the demonic world garnered through years of study, experience in thousands of deliverance cases personally conducted and deep interactions with the Holy Ghost, available unto you.

Demonology is the study of demons, their operations, manifestations, structure and characteristics. Deliverance is the process of getting rid or exorcising demons out of the life of a person, family, city or nation. This is not an exhaustive study of demonology. There is so much on demons and deliverance that we cannot put in this volume. There is so much I believe that is yet to be revealed. There is so much that we cannot bear now but the Holy Spirit will reveal more truths unto us as we fellowship with Him in our campaigns to deliver the captive from the shackles of bondage.

Why is the study of demons and the devil important?

1. Over sixty percent of the miracles of Christ in His three and a half years of ministry involved demons and deliverance. This is evidence that demonic problems are of greater proportion than any other.
2. Jesus taught in Luke 14:31 that in order to win your battle you must be able to assess and understand the strengths, strategies and techniques of your enemy.

'...*Or what king, going to make war against another king, does not sit down first and consider whether he is able with ten thousand to meet him who comes against him with twenty thousand?*

Understanding the nature of demons and their operations will enable us to avoid their traps and target our weapons more accurately.

WHO OR WHAT ARE DEMONS AND WHERE DO THEY COME FROM

Demons are disembodied spirits. They are evil spirits that have no body. In contrast, man is a spirit, he has a soul and dwells in a body. Demons are evil spirits without bodies. Consequently they cannot operate in the material world except through the possession of the bodies of men or beasts. Nevertheless they are persons; for they possess all the characteristics of personalities, and they are as varied as we are in their personalities.

WHERE DO THEY COME FROM?

1. Some fallen angels became demons when they lost their angelic bodies in the war that resulted from the rebellion of Lucifer.

According to 1 Corinthians 15:40-44, there are celestial bodies and terrestrial bodies. There are also spiritual bodies and natural bodies. These bodies have varying glories, abilities and compositions. Jesus resurrected with a glorified body, which empowered Him to appear and disappear, walk through walls and ascend unto heaven. He could also eat earthly food with that body. Angels also have glorified or heavenly bodies that empower them to perform feats impossible to the human body. I believe it is the difference in the glory, ability and composition between angelic bodies and human body that made the psalmist to declare in

1

Psalm 8:5 that man was made a little lower than the angels. It could not have been man's spirit that made him lower because man was created in the image of God.

Therefore if man is considered lower than the angels as a result of the composition of his body and we understand from Genesis 2:7 and 3:19 that the human body was made from dust then of what materials were angelic bodies made? The answer is in Ezekiel 28:13-14.

> *You were in Eden, the garden of God;*
> *Every precious stone was your covering:*
> *The sardius, topaz, and diamond,*
> *Beryl, onyx, and jasper,*
> *Sapphire, turquoise, and emerald with gold.*
> *The workmanship of your timbrels and pipes*
> *Was prepared for you on the day you were created.*
> *"You were the anointed cherub who covers;*
> *I established you;*
> *You were on the holy mountain of God;*
> *You walked back and forth in the midst of fiery stones.*

From this passage we understand that the body of Lucifer the fallen angel who became Satan was made from gold, diamonds and precious stones. If this is so it follows that most angelic bodies are made from different combinations of gold, diamonds and precious stones. It is also reasonable to infer from this that angels at creation are ranked according to the amount and type of precious stones used to make their bodies.

No wonder the Psalmist concluded that we are made a little lower than angels.

WHAT WAR?

The scriptures teach that before the creation of Adam there was war in heaven as a result of the rebellion of angel Lucifer. It was this war that made the earth without form and void in Genesis 1:2. God did not create it without form and void. He created it to be inhabited according to Isaiah 45:18. But He destroyed it when the then ruler of the earth angel Lucifer led a rebellion against the king of kings and Lord of Lords. Read the story in Isaiah 14:12 -14

> *"How you are fallen from heaven,*
> *O Lucifer, son of the morning!*
> *How you are cut down to the ground,*
> *You who weakened the nations!*
> *For you have said in your heart:*
> *'I will ascend into heaven,*
> *I will exalt my throne above the stars of God;*
> *I will also sit on the mount of the congregation*
> *On the farthest sides of the north;*
> *I will ascend above the heights of the clouds,*
> *I will be like the Most High.'*

Angel Lucifer did not rebel from heaven as some teach. He rebelled from the earth. For he said '*I will ascend into heaven*'. That means he was not in heaven when he rebelled. He was on earth as the ruler of, I believe, one third of the angels, as well as animals (maybe dinosaurs), other beings and spirits, organized into nations, cities etc. He led an army into heaven to overthrow God and a battle ensued between Lucifer's angels and God's angels. Lucifer's angels lost the battle and were kicked out of heaven hence Isaiah the prophet declared at the beginning of the quoted passage '*how you are fallen from heaven O Lucifer, son of the morning.* Outraged at Lucifer's rebellion God destroyed the earth with a flood. And some angelic bodies were destroyed beyond repair. These fallen angels whose bodies were destroyed became demons. Mark 1:23-24 proves it.

Now there was a man in their synagogue with an unclean spirit. And he cried out, saying, "Let us alone! What have we to do with You, Jesus of Nazareth? Did You come to destroy us? I know who You are—the Holy One of God!"

When I read this passage I wondered where this demon and Jesus had met before and how the unclean spirit got to know that Jesus was out to destroy him. It appears this unclean spirit was speaking out of the experience he had with the commander of the armies of heaven in battle. The battle between Lucifer's angels and God's angels before Adam was created. This unclean spirit was possibly one of the fallen angels whose body was destroyed by the power of God in that battle. So without an angelic body he becomes a demon.

2. Others were originally created without bodies as spirit aides to Lucifer and became demons (evil) when they rebelled with Lucifer.

In the book of 1Kings 22:19-23 we learnt that there are spirit aides created in spirit form (without bodies, spiritual or otherwise) who assisted God in convincing king Ahab to go to war so that he will be killed. See 1 Kings 22:19-23

Then Micaiah said, "Therefore hear the word of the LORD: I saw the LORD sitting on His throne, and all the host of heaven standing by, on His right hand and on His left. And the LORD said, 'Who will persuade Ahab to go up, that he may fall at Ramoth Gilead?' So one spoke in this manner, and another spoke in that manner. Then a spirit came forward and stood before the LORD, and said, 'I will persuade him.' "The LORD said to him, 'In what way?' So he said, 'I will go out and be a lying spirit in the mouth of all his prophets.' And the LORD said, 'You shall persuade him, and also prevail. Go out and do so.' "Therefore look! The LORD has put a lying spirit in the mouth of all these prophets of yours, and the LORD has declared disaster against you."

If God has spirit aides then it follows that while Lucifer was ruling over the earth in pre-adamic times he also could have had spirit aides who became demons when they rebelled with him. Revelation 16:13-14 confirms this.

And I saw three unclean spirits like frogs coming out of the mouth of the dragon, out of the mouth of the beast, and out of the mouth of the false prophet. For they are spirits of demons, performing signs, which go out to the kings of the earth and of the whole world, to gather them to the battle of that great day of God Almighty.

3. Giants born out of the sexual relationship of fallen angels and daughters of men according to Genesis 6:1-4, become demons when they die physically.

Now it came to pass, when men began to multiply on the face of the earth, and daughters were born to them, that the sons of God saw the daughters of men, that they were beautiful; and they took wives for themselves of all whom they chose. And the LORD said, "My Spirit shall not strive with man forever, for he is indeed flesh; yet his days shall be one hundred and twenty years." There were giants on the earth in those days, and also afterward, when the sons of God came in to the daughters of men and they bore children to them. Those were the mighty men who were of old, men of renown. Genesis 6:1-4

Comparing this passage with Job 1:6, 2:1 and 38:4-7 we understand that the phrase 'sons of God' refers to angels.

Job 1:6

Now there was a day when the sons of God came to present themselves before the LORD, and Satan also came among them.

Job 2:1
Again there was a day when the sons of God came to present themselves before the LORD, and Satan came also among them to present himself before the LORD.

Only angels are in heaven presenting themselves before the Lord.

Job 38:4-7
"Where were you when I laid the foundations of the earth?
Tell Me, if you have understanding.
Who determined its measurements?
Surely you know!
Or who stretched the line upon it?
To what were its foundations fastened?
Or who laid its cornerstone,
When the morning stars sang together,
*And all **the sons of God** shouted for joy?*

Only angels were present when the earth was being created so only them could have shouted for joy. Therefore if the 'sons of God' spoken of in Job 1:6, 2:1 and 38:7 refer to angels, then 'sons of God' in Genesis 6:1-4 could only mean angels. In fact The Living Bible translation puts Genesis 6:1-4 this way;

7

*Now a population explosion took place upon the earth. It was at this time that **beings from the spirit world** looked upon the beautiful earth women and took any they desired to be their wives. Then Jehovah said, "My Spirit must not forever be disgraced in man, wholly evil as he is. I will give him 120 years to mend his ways." In those days, and even afterwards, when the **evil beings from the spirit world** were sexually involved with human women, their children became giants, of whom so many legends are told.*

Further evidence that Genesis 6:1-4 refers to sexual relationships between fallen angels and the daughters of men can be found in Jude 6.

And the angels which kept not their first estate, but left their own habitation, he hath reserved in everlasting chains under darkness unto the judgment of the great day

Jude was saying here that certain angels were punished for not keeping their first estate and leaving their own habitation. What does he mean by that? Verse 7 of the book of Jude explains;

Even as Sodom and Gomorrha, and the cities about them in like manner, giving themselves over to fornication, and going after strange flesh, are set forth for an example, suffering the vengeance of eternal fire.

If the sin of the angels is similar to the sin of Sodom and Gomorrha then the sin of the angels was sexual. And not just sexual but going after strange flesh. Remember Sodom and Gomorrha was notorious for homosexuality (strange flesh) and even attempting to have sex with the angels sent to deliver Lot. So 'leaving their habitation' means that these fallen angels went beyond the sexual boundaries set for them by God to relate with the daughters of men.

This illicit sexual relationship gave birth to abnormally large men and women with super human strength and abilities. Men such as Goliath and Og of Bashan who were about 13 and 18 feet tall respectively. Any wonder how the Egyptian pyramids, the sphinx and other architectural wonders of old were built without modern technology? These were the legends around whom the Greek, Benin, Yoruba, Okrika etc. mythologies were formed.

However because these giants were half angels and half humans, when they died they became demons. Most testimonies of encounters with demons I have heard in many years of ministering deliverance had described the demons as unusually huge and tall. The half demon half-human concept can be related to the half fish half human concept commonly known as mermaids. Furthermore Isaiah 26:14 said this of the giants;

They are now dead, they live no more;
those departed spirits do not rise.
You punished them and brought them to ruin;
you wiped out all memory of them.

This means the giants will not attain to the resurrection of the dead unlike other dead men as verse 19 of the same chapter reveals.

> *But your dead will live;*
> *their bodies will rise.*
> *You who dwell in the dust,*
> *wake up and shout for joy.*
> *Your dew is like the dew of the morning;*
> *the earth will give birth to her dead.*

These giants are referred to as 'other lords' in verse 13 of this same chapter who had oppressed Israel;

> *O LORD, our God,* **other lords** *besides you have ruled over us, but your name alone do we honor.*

God punished the giants also known as Rephaims (translated deceased or dead in other versions see Ps 88:10-11,) by commanding Israel's kings Saul and David to wipe out their generations completely including children and livestock.

4. Human beings that are completely and consciously sold out to the devil as his agents become demons when they die physically.

Many recorded testimonies in my years of deliverance had told of a world of splendor and opulence under the sea run by demons. These testimonies have further claimed that they (the testifiers) came into this world from the sea and ought to return to the sea when they die, if they had not been delivered. Initially I was reluctant to publish these accounts because I could not substantiate these claims with scripture. But with more testimonies and more witnesses confirming these claims I couldn't ignore it anymore. So I prayerfully sought the Lord for a scriptural confirmation and the Lord answered with Revelations 20:13. Read;

'The sea gave up the dead who were in it, and Death and Hades delivered up the dead who were in them. And they were judged, each one according to his works'.

The sea gave up the dead who were in it? I thought everyone who dies goes to hell or heaven. Who are those in the sea? It couldn't be those who died on the sea, through shipwreck or other sea accidents. If it were then the scriptures should have asked for the air to give up the dead in it or the fire to give up the dead in it since some people were killed in plane crashes and others totally burnt by fire. The scriptures singled out the sea because there are spiritual kingdoms under the sea run by demons and those consciously sold out to the devil who die return there to become demons. Any wonder that the spirit of the antichrist of Revelation 13 and the spirits of the four beasts of Daniel 7 representing the gentile empires of prophecy came out of the sea. In fact Revelation 13:1 says that the spirit of the antichrist came out of the sea to take on the body of a man while verse 11 says the spirit of the prophet of the antichrist came out of the earth. This contrast shows that the sea in Revelation 13:1 means

11

more than just the sea of humanity as some theologians had postulated in the past. Following is one of the many testimonies confirming the existence of a world under the sea.

MARINE UNDERWORLD

My name is Blessing. I was initiated into the marine world during the new yam festival when a witch doctor performed certain rituals with the blood of sacrificed animals. Some of that blood was sprinkled on my head while some of it was used to prepare my meals. According to the witch doctor I came into this physical world from the marine underworld hence I deserve to be treated with the reverent difference accorded such people. Consequently these rituals continued regularly until I was eight years old when my parents became born again.

Once the rituals stopped the torment began. The powers of darkness seem to be expressing their displeasure at my parent's rebellion. I was afflicted with all manners of ailments that defied treatment. I began to have vivid and frightening encounters with the marine world.

Leonard came into my life about this time. We were colleagues at the same primary school. One day he took me to a riverbank and had sex with me. I felt powerless to resist him. With the benefit of hindsight, I believe I was hypnotized. I did not understand it then because I was so young and innocent. When after the sexual intercourse, we proceeded into the river, it seemed the most natural thing to follow him without question. We spent three days inside the river.

It was an entirely different world. We went deep into the river until we got underneath the water. As we approached, I was stunned to see so many people. There were men, women and children of different shades and character. A huge crowd had gathered. They were the welcome party.

Apparently my arrival was anticipated. The queen of the coast who told me how delighted she was that I could make it specially welcomed me. After the welcome ceremonies I was given blood to drink to establish my membership. Though no one told me, some how I knew that I dared not refuse the blood because the consequences of such an act could only be imagined.

Then a man named Belial arrived. The usual thinking among most people is that devils are ugly, black with pointed tails, stumpy horns and carry pitch forks. That is not correct. Belial was a light complexioned handsome man without any hint of the wickedness associated with him. The kind of man many women find irresistible. The queen, the dominant personality in the gathering announced that I was now due for marriage. Belial promptly staked his claim by declaring his intention to marry me.

Before the marriage could take place however I was asked to go back into the world and ruin lives, cause confusion and generally wreck havoc, the magnitude of which will determine my suitability as the wife of such an exalted one as Belial. To accomplish my assignments, I was adequately armed.

Meanwhile my parents did not suspect anything was wrong except when I drum up all kinds of flimsy excuses to avoid church. They however were concerned when they noticed certain physical changes in my body. Some weeks I will look very ugly and at other times I will look very beautiful.

September 4th 1993, I relocated to Lagos, Nigeria and there I ran into Leonard again after a few years. We met at a friend's party by what I thought was a mere coincidence. Until this time we had not been in contact.

At the party Leonard requested that we go for a walk along the beach. I obliged again powerless to resist him. As we walked along the beach, we played catch up, enjoying the sea breeze and each other's company.

Suddenly I looked towards the sea and saw a female figure rise out of the sea and sort of glide towards us. As she approached I observed that she was a mermaid. I froze in fear and instantly she was close enough to wipe my face with her hand. With that my fear disappeared and I followed her into the depths. By this time Leonard had simply varnished.

The usual crowd gathered once again at our arrival but the mood was different. I was welcomed and given a special seat, like a throne. I was then crowned and made ready for marriage to Belial. Belial arrived and the marriage was immediately consummated after which I was given several gifts and powers.

I was given three types of sex organs. One of a serpent, one of a scorpion and one of a fish. I was also

14

given rings, beads and special underwear. With the rings on my fingers all I need to do is tap a man on the shoulder three times and he would be at my beck and call. While wearing the beads on my waist I could sleep with several men in a day with minimal discomfort. My sexual prowess was enhanced. The special underwear made me irresistible to men. They were drawn to me as if hypnotized.

The three types of sex organs were used for different purposes. The one of a serpent was for ruining a man's business or finances. Any wealthy man who slept with me was certain to become poor. That of a scorpion was used to punish men who refuse to give in to my demands for money, jewelry or any other desire. As soon as they sleep with me they become terminally ill. That of the fish was used to initiate men into the marine world. A man who sleeps with me is hooked. All the powers of darkness need to do is to reel him in. You can't begin to imagine all the men, and businesses and homes that I ruined with these powers. Thank God for the blood of Jesus that has washed away my sins.

I had entered into a covenant with Belial that I would never have children in the physical. If for any reason I become pregnant I will die during labor. **Part of the terms of the covenant also stated that I would only remain on earth for twenty-eight years, after which I would return permanently to the water.**

However I gave birth to spiritual children for Belial. My first child named Vivian was born when I was thirteen years old. Two other children - Deborah and Celia followed in rapid succession. Strangely *enough whenever I was pregnant for Belial, my monthly menstrual cycle will cease in the physical for nine months. It is these spiritual children (half demons/human) that are given to these women that go look for children from witch doctors. And for those children there is always a demonic agenda for their untimely return to the water.*

On the 18th of January 2000 I met Christ when a sister invited me to your church and my whole life was transformed. I was taken through intense deliverance during a seven-day prayer and fasting period and today I am free from Belial, marine spirits and all the powers of Darkness. Praise God!

Seven important truths about demons

1. They possess intelligence, knowledge and wisdom. 1kings 22:19-24; Matthew 8:26-33; Luke 4:41; Acts 19:15; Mark 1:23-26.

2. They have individual wills, feelings, emotions, desires and other soul and spirit faculties. Mark 5:7; 16:9; Matthew 8:28-31; 12:43-45; Acts 8:7;

3. They have supernatural strength and miraculous powers. Mark 5:1-18; Revelation 16:13-14;

4. They use the bodies and physical organs of those they are permitted to operate in to carry out every physical, mental, emotional and social activity that they desire. Mark 1:23-34; 5:7-12; Matthew 12:43-45; 1Timothy 4:1;

1Samuel 28:3-19; 1Chronicles 10:13; Isaiah 8:19; Deuteronomy 18:11;

5. They use human bodies for security, protection and rest. Matthew 12:43-45; 8:28-32; Mark 5:7-13; Luke 8:26-33;

6. There are demons for every sickness, disease, affliction, torment, unholy trait and doctrinal error known to man. 2Chronicles 33:6; 1Samuel 18.8-11; Matthew 4:23-24; 9:32-33; 12:22; 13:36-43; 15:22; 17:15-16; Mark 9:20; Luke 4:36; 11:26; John 8:44; Acts 10:38; 16:16-18; Romans 8:15; 1Corinthians 2:12; 2Timothy 1:7; 1John 4:1-6;

7. Demons are transferable through inheritance and sex. Genesis 6:1-7; Deuteronomy 5:9; Exodus 20:5; 1Corinthians 6:16-18;

<u>HOW IT ALL BEGAN</u>

The Garden of Eden. Genesis 2:25-3:24

When God reconstructed the earth, planted the Garden of Eden and placed Adam in it to exercise dominion and rule, demons and the devil existed but had no direct access to Adam. This is because God made the natural world in such a way that it was impossible for the devil to communicate with man without the use of a physical body. The devil could not project thoughts, send evil pictures into Adam's imagination or even invade his dream life because there were no parameters in Adam's heart by which he could recognize such influences, for Adam was created without the knowledge of evil. There were no databases or information systems in Adams heart by which he could measure, discern, acknowledge or recognize evil. He was innocent and incapable of imagining or thinking up anything evil. His entire knowledge of wrong consists only of eating or not eating the fruit of the tree of the knowledge of good and evil. And he was incapable of the thought of disobeying that command unless an external being physically spoke that suggestion into his hearing. Such was their innocence that they were naked and did not even know it and so were incapable of being ashamed of it. (Genesis 2:25; 3:7,10,11;).

In other words Adam was created without a conscience.

ADAM CREATED WITHOUT A CONSCIENCE?

Yes! Conscience is a sense of right and wrong. It is a standard in our minds against which our thoughts and actions are measured for approval or condemnation. It is the knowledge of good and evil. Adam had no conscience when he was initially created because he had no knowledge of evil. He was created to be ruled, directed and guided by his spirit, which was in perfect union with the spirit of God. That is why 1 Corinthians 6:17 says, *'but he that is joined unto the Lord is one spirit'.* In this state God is completely trusted. God is the standard. Man does not have the capacity to evaluate the decisions of God. Man does not seek knowledge of available options. The only option is God. Everything from God is blindly accepted whether we understand it or not. This is God's perfect will. Adam received conscience, when he ate of the tree of knowledge of good and evil. In fact he acquired conscience by eating of the tree of Knowledge of good and evil. No wonder it was called the tree of knowledge of good and evil. Notice that the tree of the knowledge of good and evil was not a bad tree or it would not have been in the Garden of Eden. Because everything God created he declared that it was good. The tree of the knowledge of good and evil was only another option permitted by God in other to give man a choice. Therefore conscience is God's permissive will for ruling the man, that is if the conscience is still pure and had not been polluted, seared or mortgaged. For conscience is not as constant and unchangeable as the spirit of the living God. (See

1Timothy 1:5,19; 3:9; 4:2; 2Timothy 1:3; Acts 23:1; 24:16; Hebrews 9:9,14; 10:2,22; 13:18; Titus 1:15; 1Corinthians 8:7,10,12; 1Peter 2:19; 3:16,21; Romans 2:12-15; 9:1.)

Since it was not possible for the devil to break into the world of Adam and communicate with him directly, (I believe he couldn't even enter the Garden of Eden; he must have met the snake outside the garden). He sought for a body through which to break the communication barrier and found that body in the snake who yielded unto him perhaps because he (the devil) was a superior being. Clothed with the body of the snake the devil headed back into Eden and using the faculties of the snake opened up a discourse with Eve that resulted in the fall. It was for allowing itself to be used of the devil to break the communication barrier between Adam and the devil that the snake was cursed in *Genesis 3:14.*

> *So the LORD God said to the serpent, "Because*
> *you have done this,*
> *"Cursed are you above all the livestock*
> *and all the wild animals!*
> *You will crawl on your belly*
> *and you will eat dust*
> *all the days of your life.*

Obviously this is not a curse on the devil because the devil is not an animal or livestock and is not presently crawling on his belly, which would have been the case if this curse was upon the devil. Rather it is the snake that now crawls on his belly and eats dust.

But the following verse is a curse on the devil and a prophecy of the victory of Christ over the devil.

> *Genesis 3:15*
> *"And I will put enmity*
> *between you and the woman,*
> *and between your offspring and hers;*
> *he will crush your head,*
> *and you will strike his heel."*

Christ did not fight the snake, he fought the devil and defeated him in hell through His death and resurrection. Colossians 2:15; Hebrew 2:14-15;

Demonic consequences of the fall

1. Man became a slave of demons. Demons can now possess, oppress, afflict, torment, inhabit and cohabit man at will. If this is true, then is there any unbeliever that is not demonized? John 8:34; Matthew 12:43-45;

2. The communication barrier was broken. Demons now have access to man's mind. They can project thoughts and influence man's thinking even without indwelling the man. Man now has the parameters or database to recognize evil; the knowledge of good and evil or conscience if you will.

3. Demons can now use man's body not only to express themselves but also to limit, hinder and prevent man from attaining unto God's ideal.

21

Man's body became a weapon in the hands of demons against man. Galatians 5:16-17; Romans 7:15-24.

Needless to say that Adam immediately after the fall became possessed by demons. Some of the demonic spirits that manifested through Adam's body immediately he sinned include the spirits of; fear, shame, inadequacy, slander, lying, rebellion, idolatry, rejection, lust, manipulation, death, hindrance, pain, pride, selfishness, irresponsibility, etc.

Kinds of demonization

1. *Possession:* This is the complete ownership and control of an individual by demon spirits. It is not very common to find people who are possessed in this sense, for even those that are insane have their sane moments. Of course there are those who are completely sold out to the devil. Who do his bidding every moment but the fact that some of them get born again is evidence that they do exercise their individual will sometimes. They may be owned by the devil but not controlled by the devil twenty-four hours a day and seven days a week. All unbelievers are owned by the devil but not all of them are totally controlled by the devil. Ownership is the right to exercise control, which is different from the actual exercise of that control. Born again children of God are not

owned by the devil although aspects of their lives could be controlled by the devil. Nevertheless possession is more commonly used to define the degree of demonization. In fact the literal meaning of the Greek word (daimonizomai) used in the scriptures to define possession is 'to be under the power of a demon.' In this sense possession is common and can be graduated according to the degree to which we are under the power of a demon. For instance we experience momentary possession when the spirit of anger takes over our psyches and we lash out in uncontrollable rage. According to Faussets Bible dictionary, a possessed man has lost the power of individual will and reason. His personal consciousness becomes strangely confused with that of a demon so as to produce a twofold will. Possessed persons irrespective of the degree usually have at least a demon or an unclean spirit living or inhabiting there bodies. Possession is the highest form of demonization.

2. *Oppression:* This is an even more common form of demonization particularly in the church. When we or certain aspects of our lives are dominated or bound by demon oppression is in place. In the case of oppression the demons may not be necessarily living in the body of the oppressed person but they have a relationship that gives them access to go in and out. Usually the demons would have deposited properties and created habits, sicknesses and

strongholds (defenses) which like a magnet attracts them back and guarantees them access at will. These deposits, habits and strongholds become spiritual burdens, chains and yokes that hinder us from becoming or achieving God's best for us. For instance a slanderous or lying spirit could oppress someone's tongue. Or someone could be oppressed by a spirit of depression or someone's womb oppressed by a spiritual husband through miscarriages.

3. *Obsession:* This is a form of demonization that attaches itself to the mind and emotions. It refers to an uncontrollable devotion or attachment to something or someone. An exclusive and complete occupation of the faculties of the soul. It is a relationship that allows a demon spirit to seize one's mind sometimes with an overpowering thought and weaken the power of the will concerning the object of obsession. It is sometimes an expression of unholy soul-ties and breeds the spirits of fear, jealousy, anxiety, manipulation, intimidation and control (jezebel spirits). In this form of demonization, the obsessed person is haunted and completely besieged by demons usually camped around his spiritual space bombarding him with oppressive and overpowering thoughts and feelings concerning the object of obsession that completely seals off every contrary reasoning. E.g. pornography, ouiija board etc. Obsession is a form of idolatry.

4. *Affliction:* Demons sometimes attack and impose severe distress, pain, suffering, sickness, disease and torment on people. This is usually an external attack through spells, enchantments, incantations and spiritual exposure. In this form of demonization the spirits gain access to the spiritual environment of the afflicted person through disobedience, carelessness, traitors or the law of sowing and reaping, and cause suffering. Usually there is a magnet inside that allows the attack to be effective. Spiritual leeches, parasites, webs, weights and shadows arise through this form of demonization. Horoscope, palmistry, psychics, divination, false prophecy attract afflictions to patrons.

DEMONIC OPERATIONS

Crossbreeding of angels and man to produce Giants. Genesis 6:1-4

":1 Now it came to pass, when men began to multiply on the face of the earth, and daughters were born to them, 2 that the sons of God saw the daughters of men, that they were beautiful; and they took wives for themselves of all whom they chose. 3 And the LORD said, "My Spirit shall not strive with man forever, for he is indeed flesh; yet his days shall be one hundred and twenty years." 4 There were giants on the

earth in those days, and also afterward, when the sons of God came in to the daughters of men and they bore children to them. Those were the mighty men who were of old, men of renown.

1. The fall of Adam gave the devil the legal basis to inhabit man's body but the devil wanted more. He wanted to completely pollute the bloodline of Adam so that it will be impossible for the seed of the woman promised in Genesis 3:15 to be born without having some demonic genes. In other words Satan wanted to create a hybrid, devil-man, race by having fallen angels, (called sons of God here) relate sexually with women. If this is so then not everybody is human. Some people walking or living around us could be devil-men. Hear Matthew 13:24-26, 37-39;

Jesus told them another parable: "The kingdom of heaven is like a man who sowed good seed in his field. 25 But while everyone was sleeping, his enemy came and sowed weeds among the wheat, and went away. 26 When the wheat sprouted and formed heads, then the weeds also appeared...

37 He answered, "The one who sowed the good seed is the Son of Man. 38 The field is the world, and the good seed stands for the sons of the kingdom. The weeds are the sons of the evil one, 39 and the enemy who sows them is the devil. The harvest is the end of the age, and the harvesters are angels.

(Also see, Job 1:6; 2:1; 38:7; Daniel 3:25,28; Jude 6-7.)

2. The result was the birth of giants. Men with super-human strengths and abilities and abnormal body sizes and features. Some had 6 fingers on each hand and 6 toes on each foot. Goliath was about 13 feet tall. Og, king of Bashan was described as a giant whose bed was about 18 feet long and 8 feet wide. Some of these giants became gods and deities worshipped by localities and tribes and form the basis of tribal myths such as the Yoruba, Benin, Okrika and Greek mythologies. Genesis 6:4; Deuteronomy 3:11; 1Samuel 17:4-6; 2Samuel 21:16-22; 1Chronicles 20:4-8;

3. It was because of this pollution of the Adamite stock that the world of Noah was destroyed by flood. Nevertheless the pollution continued after the flood. Consequent upon this amongst other reasons God instructed the Israelites never to marry outside Israel and to utterly destroy all the inhabitants of Canaan when they possess the Land. Genesis 6:4; 19:1-9; Exodus 34:11-16; Deuteronomy 7:1-5;

4. The fallen angels that participated in this crossbreeding abomination were immediately punished by God and reserved in everlasting chains under darkness until the Judgment day. Jude 6-7; 2Peter 2:4; Revelation 20:11-15;

5. The concept of spiritual husband/wife where people have sex in the dream or semi-reality with spirit beings sometimes masquerading as familiar faces, which is common today, originated from this

cross breeding of Genesis 6. As earlier proven these spiritual husbands/wives are the giants who died long ago and became demons. Isaiah 26:14.

6. The half-human, half-fallen angel concept can be related to the half fish, half-human concept commonly known as mermaids.

STRUCTURE, HIERARCHY AND ORGANIZATION OF THE KINGDOM OF DARKNESS

Ephesians 6:12
'For we do not wrestle against flesh and blood, but against principalities, against powers, against the rulers of the darkness of this age, against spiritual hosts of wickedness in the heavenly places.

Satan is at the head of a massive demonic organization, (I believe the same structure through which he ruled the earth in pre-adamic times), hierarchically and systematically structured to frustrate the counsel and purposes of God. Ephesians 6:12 reveal the following levels of authority in the demonic realm;

PRINCIPALITIES

These are the chief princes, chief ministers, chief rulers, next in rank to Satan himself, with great spheres of influence beyond national and continental borders. They deputize for Satan himself and constitute his board of directors. There are at least four principalities that we can recognize in the scriptures and these include:

1. *Death;* The last enemy to be destroyed. One of his chief lieutenants is Hades. Revelation 6:8; 20:14; 1Corinthians 15:26;

2. *Beast or Antichrist;* The world dictator of the tribulation years who will lead the armies of the world against Israel, Christ and the raptured saints at the battle of Armageddon. Revelation 6:2; 13:1-18; 16:13-16; 19:19-20;

3. *Abaddon or Apollyon;* This is the angel of the bottomless pit who is also referred to as the angel of destruction or destroyer. He is a fallen angel and the king of the wild demonic creatures that will be released in the tribulation years to torment the earth. I believe the four fallen angels presently bound in river Euphrates who command the two hundred million demon horsemen prepared for the destruction of thirty three percent of mankind during the great tribulation are some of the chief lieutenants of this principality. Revelation 9:1-19;

4. *Belial:* This is the architect of wickedness, insanity, foolishness, perversity etc. I believe he is currently the pseudo ruler or Prime Minister of Satan. 2Corinthians 6:15; Judges 19:22; 1Kings 21:13; 2Samuel 23:6; 1Samuel 30:22;

POWERS

These are next in rank to the principalities and derive their authority from the principalities. They are departmental heads with spheres of influence across national and even continental boundaries who execute the will and plans of the principalities. Some of the powers we can recognize from scripture include;

1. *Mammon:* The god of money. His lieutenants include devourer, poverty, stinginess, etc. Matthew 6:24; Luke 16:13; Malachi 3:11; Proverbs 6:11; 24:34;
2. *Gog and Magog:* The powers in charge of war. Revelation 6:4; 20:8; Ezekiel 38:2; 39:6;
3. *Baal, Baalzebub:* The power in charge of false religion. Numbers 25:3; Judges 6:25; 1Kings. 16:32; 18:21; Matthew 12:24;
4. *Ashtoreth:* The goddess of sex, sensuality, fertility, and the moon. Isis, Ishtar, Venus, Diana are other names or expressions of this power. Judges 2:13; 10:6;
5. *Hades:* The chief lieutenant of death. Revelation 6:8; 20:14;
6. *The four angels bound at river Euphrates who commands the 200 million demonic army of Revelation 9:14-17.*

I believe there are more powers in the scriptures than these mentioned here.

RULERS OF DARKNESS

These are the territorial powers that administer the various hemispheres, continents, regions, nations, states, counties, cities, neighborhoods, streets and houses on behalf of Satan. In the same way that we have various levels of government and rulership in the natural, Satan has set up his own administration over the earth in the spiritual. Though the earth was destroyed in pre-adamic times I believe Satan did not dismantle his administrative structure through which he governed then. They still exercised their hegemonies over vast territories from the heavenlies. In other words every geographical region, nation, state, county, city, neighborhood, street, block, building has a demonic power or ruler of darkness exercising dominion over it. Unless believers counter that authority in prayer. An example of a ruler of darkness is the prince of Persia in Daniel 10:13-21. These rulers of darkness are sometimes the powers behind the throne, presidency, governorship or mayoralty of that territory. This was more apparent in the days of monarchies when single families rule a particular territory for ages. Oftentimes these rulers of darkness will employ supernatural powers to raise up their candidates in the natural to seize power through violence or democratic processes in order to carry out their agenda in that nation. This is the plan of the devil for the end times when he will raise up a world dictator in the form of the anti-christ to implement his agenda for the world. This is why Jesus said in Mark 3:27:

'No one can enter a strong man's house and plunder his goods, unless he first binds the strong man. And then he will plunder his house.

We must understand that it is necessary for us believers to exercise our dominion over every geographical area where we operate in the natural daily. Nations, cities, streets have been denied revival because we have failed to first bind the rulers of darkness in charge of those places. We had not been able to realize our full potential in certain places where we had gone to preach or do business because we never took charge of that territory through fasting and prayer. Ezekiel 28:12; 2Thessalonians 2:7; Matthew 16:19; Luke 10:19; Ephesians 6:12;

SPIRITS OF WICKEDNESS IN HEAVENLY PLACES

These are the spirits that actually execute the wicked plans of Satan and his cohorts. They include the following:

1. *spirits of infirmities:* These are the spirits responsible for diseases and illnesses such as the spirit of cancer, diabetes, blindness, deaf/dumb, paralysis, insanity etc. I believe all sicknesses and diseases are caused by demon spirits although eating the wrong thing or poor maintenance of our body could be the trigger that allowed the demon spirit to afflict or plant the sickness. This position is based on the truth that sickness, which is death in process, came into the world as a result of sin. So if there had not been sin then what we eat or do not eat,

whether we exercise or not would not have mattered since we could not be sick. In other words if Adam had not sinned and then went without sleeping for three days he would not have a headache. Or if he ate sugar every day he would not be at the risk of diabetes because these sicknesses did not exist in his world. Luke 13:10-16; Mk. 9:25;

2. *Mermaid/Marine/Water Spirits:* These refer to a group of spirits connected with springs, lakes, rivers, seas and sea creatures. They are prevalent in areas where there is a lot of water. In fact they live in the waters and have kingdoms and cities there. Any wonder then that the beast of Revelation 13 comes out of the sea. Revelation 13:1,11; 20:13;

3. *Familiar Spirits:* these groups of spirits are usually from the land; hills, forests, graves etc. They include divination, necromancy, astrology, enchantments and spells. They also include what Africans call ogbanje or emere spirits. Deuteronomy 18:10-11; Leviticus 19:26,31; 20:6,27;

4. *Controlling or Jezebel Spirits:* These are the manipulating, intimidating, seducing and provoking spirits. They are also known as witchcraft spirits. They include all forms of sorcery, voodoo etc. Deuteronomy 8:10-11;

5. *Occult Spirits:* These spirits arise out of idol worship, false religion, intellectual cults etc.

6. *Animal Spirits:* These are demons that have taken on animal forms, characteristics or manifestations. They result from animal worship and from crossbreeding of animals with demons. Some of the spirits in this class include, snake spirits, cat spirits, dog spirits, fox spirits, hyena spirits, turtle spirits, vulture spirits etc. Genesis 3:1;

7. *Sin Spirits:* These are spirits of sin such as lying spirit, slandering spirits, lust spirits, unforgiving spirits, adulterous spirits, murderous spirits, suicide spirits, spirits of rejection, inferiority, low self esteem, depression, pride, rebellion, unbelief etc. 1Kings 22:22; John 8:34; Romans 7:14-25; 8:2;

A CITY IN AN ANTHILL

TESTIMONY OF A DEMONIZED WOMAN - MAMA TOYIN

When my father failed to produce children by his first six wives, he married my mother as the seventh. She already had a son by her first marriage, so it was expected that she would bear children with my dad. Initially she did not and it became obvious that my dad was the impotent one. At this point they approached the goddess of "Ari-oyin" river and offered sacrifices of appeasement and my mother became pregnant that month. Nine months later I emerged. From then, the following rituals were religiously observed. I was bathed only with cold water. No hot water touches me. Hence I was popularly referred to as "Olomi tutu".

Every eight days since birth I must be taken to that river along with all the other children sourced from that river. Our mothers usually came naked, carrying large pots on their heads with which to fetch water. They would sing praises to the goddess of the river who would then appear physically. She was a very large fish. All the children irrespective of age are then thrown into the river along with the sacrifices (usually edibles) for the goddess to play and dance with. Once she was satisfied she would varnish into the deep and fresh water will spring out of the deep. This was what our mothers fetched for bathing, drinking and medicinal purposes.

When I became an adolescent I was not taken to the river again because by now I had an 'Emere' (familiar spirit) group to which I belonged. We usually met in an anthill. Whenever my mother sent me to retail food (rice and beans) I would take the food to this anthill, knock at a door not visible to the natural eyes and the anthill would open up to reveal a very beautiful and technologically advanced city. The ruling power in that city was our spiritual mother, an unusually large women with multiple breasts all over her body. She gives herbal and demonic prescriptions through witch doctors to solve problems she originally created and receives a large portion of all the sacrifices offered to witch doctors and herbalists. She would welcome me gladly take reports of my other family and buy all the food for the children in the city to eat. And I could return home anytime I please.

Once my father offended me and I stayed in the anthill for seven days to punish him. Every one was searching for me and the police were alerted. I saw all their activities from the anthill. Sometimes I visited my house unseen to the natural eyes. However I returned on the seventh day when I saw how disturbed my mother was.

At marriage my participation in the familiar spirit group reduced drastically. Then I began to experience difficulties in my marriage, finances, health etc. My money would disappear mysteriously. My merchandise and jewelry too, without a trace. My health deteriorated greatly and my children rebelled against me. Life was miserable. Child bearing was initially difficult. The minimum age difference between my children is ten years. Then I began to seek for solutions to my problem. I went from one witch doctor to another, one church to another until I found Jesus and made him the Lord of my life. I went through deliverance and was set free and the miraculous began to happen in my life regularly.

DELIVERANCE

Deliverance is a process that begins with knowledge and involves:

1. Diagnosis:-   Discerning the spirits in operation.
2. Treatment:-   Casting out the demons
3. Management:-   Maintaining the deliverance or keeping the demons out.

DIAGNOSIS

…to another discerning of spirits,
1Corinthians 12:10

This describes the process by which demonic problems, their source and the spirits in operation are recognized and identified. This process is essential for effective treatment because without accurate diagnosis we may fight as those that beat the air. Demons thrive in ignorance. They hate the light and do not want you to know what they are up to. Or if you know blame it on someone else, Aunt Jesse or Cousin Joe. As long as you do not suspect them your bullets will be off target. Knowledge of the kind of enemy you are fighting is essential for victory. So is knowledge of the weapons available unto us through Christ Jesus. And this knowledge must be available to both the deliverance minister and the patient. Oftentimes people that have been delivered in the past fail to maintain their deliverance because they did not know what they were delivered from in the first place and so could not avoid the pitfalls that allowed the demons in initially. I once cast out a spirit that had entered a lady through the possession of property dedicated to idols without disclosing the diagnosis to her and the demon came back because the property in question was not destroyed after the deliverance.

HOW DEMONS ENTER

Demons do not dwell in our spirits (the Holy Ghost dwells there if we are born again), they dwell in our bodies and in our spiritual space. Man is a spirit. He has a soul and dwells in a body. Our bodies are like houses and are capable of accommodating more than one spirit. The Gadarene demoniac in Mark chapter 5, had 6000 unclean spirits dwelling in him besides his own spirit. Even if you are born again. You get born again in your spirit. Your body never gets born again until it is redeemed at the rapture or resurrection. (Romans 8:23; Ephesians 1:14). At the point of salvation your spirit man is regenerated or made alive again by the Holy Spirit because it was dead having been separated from God. The Holy Spirit becomes one with your spirit man and dwells there, (1Corinthians 6:17), while demons dwell in your body. It is like having roaches, termites, mice and other insects living together with you in the same house. You may or may not be aware of their presence until you discover their destructive acts. And they could not have gotten into your house unless there was an opening. Demons do not enter and abide in a person unless there is an opening. Some of the ways through which demons enter into our lives include sin, curses, covenants, unholy soul-ties, spells, yokes and enchantments, incisions and tattoos etc.

Sin

Jesus answered them, "Most assuredly, I say to you, whoever commits sin is a slave of sin. John 8:34.

Everyone who commits sin is a slave of sin. Therefore whenever we sin we open ourselves up to be inhabited by demons. If you lie, you become a slave of the lying spirit and that spirit and his cohorts can indwell you. If you worship an idol you become a slave of the spirit behind that idol and that spirit can indwell you. If you are unforgiving you open yourself up to the spirits of bitterness, anger, hatred, slander, murder, witchcraft, rebellion, stubbornness, manipulation, jezebel etc. Given this fact it is not erroneous to postulate that all unbelievers are demonized. Nevertheless some demon spirits do leave at the point of salvation. Romans 6:16;

Don't you know that when you offer yourselves to someone to obey him as slaves, you are slaves to the one whom you obey-whether you are slaves to sin, which leads to death, or to obedience, which leads to righteousness?

Curses

A curse is an invocation of harm against a person, group, family, generations, city, tribe, state, nation, peoples or continent. It is the opposite of a blessing and has the potential to cause that harm invoked on that person. Whether spoken or written a curse opens the door for demons to enter into our lives. This is because curses whether imposed by God, man or the devil, are enforced by demons. As angels are the enforcers of blessings even so demons are the enforcers of curses. For instance if a curse of poverty is pronounced on someone, the enforcer of that curse is the spirit of poverty. That curse gives the spirit of poverty the right to live and operate in the life of that person. A curse of failure or death on a person gives the spirits of failure or death access to the lives of that person. A witch doctor cursed his wife and a tormenting spirit entered into her life and took away her sleep and her peace. A neighbor cursed another woman over some dispute and a strange object began to move around inside the woman's body. The men of a family cursed with death all died before a particular age and in similar circumstances or of the same illness. Whenever a particular pattern of misfortune is observable in the life of a group or family a curse is in operation. Curses could be inflicted by God, the devil, man, those in spiritual authority over us or by ourselves.

41

David Okumgba

THE LAW OF COMPOUND PUNISHMENT FOR SIN:

Every sin attracts compound punishment; it attracts an eternal or spiritual punishment and a punishment in this life. The eternal punishment is death or hell and the natural punishment is a curse. Thus every sin attracts a curse. In the same way every act of righteousness attracts an eternal reward and a reward in this life. Hear Mark 10:29-30

"So Jesus answered and said, "Assuredly, I say to you, there is no one who has left house or brothers or sisters or father or mother or wife or children or lands, for My sake and the gospel's, who shall not receive a hundredfold now in this time—houses and brothers and sisters and mothers and children and lands, with persecutions—and in the age to come, eternal life.

The blessings and curses of Deuteronomy chapter 28 are natural blessings and curses, they are not eternal. When Adam sinned in Genesis chapter 3 he received both punishments. Chapter 2 and verse 17 declares the eternal punishment;

"but of the tree of the knowledge of good and evil you shall not eat, for in the day that you eat of it you shall surely die."

While chapter 3 verses 16 through 19 captures the curse;

To the woman He said:

"I will greatly multiply your sorrow and your conception;

In pain you shall bring forth children;

Your desire shall be for your husband,

And he shall rule over you."

Then to Adam He said, "Because you have heeded the voice of your wife, and have eaten from the tree of which I commanded you, saying, 'You shall not eat of it':

"Cursed is the ground for your sake;

In toil you shall eat of it

All the days of your life.

Both thorns and thistles it shall bring forth for you,

And you shall eat the herb of the field.

In the sweat of your face you shall eat bread

Till you return to the ground,

For out of it you were taken;

For dust you are,

And to dust you shall return."

Similarly when King David sinned in 2 Samuel chapter 12 by killing Uriah and taking his wife, his punishment was compounded. Although he was forgiven of the eternal punishment in verse 13;

So David said to Nathan, "I have sinned against the LORD." And Nathan said to David, "The LORD also has put away your sin; you shall not die.

Yet the curse in verses 10, 11, 12 and 14 remained;

"Now therefore, the sword shall never depart from your house, because you have despised Me, and have taken the wife of Uriah the Hittite to be your wife.' 11 "Thus says the LORD: 'Behold, I will raise up adversity against you from your own house; and I will take your wives before your eyes and give them to your neighbor, and he shall lie with your wives in the sight of this sun. For you did it secretly, but I will do this thing before all Israel, before the sun.'

However, because by this deed you have given great occasion to the enemies of the LORD to blaspheme, the child also who is born to you shall surely die."

These curses were fulfilled in, the death of the child, the incest of Amnon and his murder by Absalom, Absalom's rebellion and incest with king David's wives in public and subsequent death in battle. 2Samuel 12:15-18:33;

The foregoing scriptures show that when we sin and we repent we are forgiven the eternal punishment however it appears the curse remains until we break it and cast out of our lives the demons responsible for enforcing those curses. In the case of King David I want to believe that he tried to break those curses but he did not succeed. Why? Was it because he did not have the blood of Jesus yet? Or was it the law of sowing and reaping in operation? Or was it some form of chastening as suggested by Hebrew 12:5-11;

Numbers 14:18; Exodus 34:7; 2Samuel 21:1-14; 24:1-18; 1kings 21:17-29; Galatians 6:7; Genesis 8:22;

Throughout scripture evidence abounds to prove that though God forgives he nevertheless chastens those he loves. In other words when we sin and repent God forgives us and we are spared from eternal damnation, nevertheless our sin has set in motion some natural consequences that may bring chastisements or trials unto us or to our children, because of the law of sowing and reaping. God will now use these same trials and chastisements to remold or promote us while graciously providing a way of escape.

THE POWER OF RESTITUTION:

Do not be deceived, God is not mocked; for whatever a man sows, that he will also reap. Galatians 6:7;

According to the law of sowing and reaping everything we do or say is a seed that will bring forth a harvest after its kind. So if we sow seeds of discord we will reap discord. If we sow seeds of greed we will reap in like manner. In fact we even reap harvests of seeds sown by our forbears whether good or bad. So what happens when we repent? Is the evil seed automatically destroyed? If that is the case why did king Ahaziah reap the harvest of his father, Ahab's seed even after Ahab had repented in 1kings 21:27-29?

'So it was, when Ahab heard those words, that he tore his clothes and put sackcloth on his body, and

fasted and lay in sackcloth, and went about mourning. And the word of the LORD came to Elijah the Tishbite, saying, "See how Ahab has humbled himself before Me? Because he has humbled himself before Me, I will not bring the calamity in his days. In the days of his son I will bring the calamity on his house."

Or why didn't king David's repentance in 2Samuel 12:13 cancel the seed of death and save the life of his son by Uriah's wife? The scriptures are clear; whatever a man's sows he shall reap. However in 2Samuel chapter 21 there is a story demonstrating the power of restitution to destroy negative seeds. In this story there was famine in the land and on king David's inquiry the Lord revealed that it was because king Saul broke the treaty Joshua made with the Gibeonites by killing them. King David restituted by giving the Gibeonites seven sons of Saul and the famine stopped. I believe that restitution destroys negative seeds and prevents them from reproducing after its kind in our lives. However for the things that cannot be restituted if we have truly repented God will give the grace to endure the unpleasant harvest; a form of chastening or trial that produces perseverance, character, hope and the peaceable fruit of righteousness.

WAY OF ESCAPE:

No temptation has overtaken you except such as is common to man; but God is faithful, who will not allow you to be tempted beyond what you are able,

***but with the temptation will also make the way of
escape, that you may be able to bear it. 1Corinthians.
10:13;***

God does not reverse His word but He provides a
way of escape for every trial. For instance 'the soul
that sins shall die' but if we appeal to the blood of
Jesus we shall live. When Adam sinned God provided
a way of escape in animal sacrifices which it self is a
shadow of Christ. When the generation of Noah sinned
God provided a way of escape in the Ark. At the
plagues in Egypt God provided a way of escape
through the Passover lamb. When the Israelites
murmured against Moses and God sent fiery serpents
to kill the people, God also provided a way of escape
in the bronze serpent. At the destruction of Jericho
God provided a way of escape for Rahab through the
Scarlet thread. When king David numbered the people
contrary to the will of God and a plague resulted, God
provided a way of escape by instructing David to build
an altar at the threshing floor of Araunah and offer
sacrifices there. As a king God's word is irreversible or
it will be worthless. Has he spoken it? Will He not do
it? Nevertheless in His mercy he provides us with a
way out of that trial, curse, temptation or situation.
Genesis 3:21; 6:1-22; Exodus 12:23; Numbers 21:4-9;
23:19-20; Joshua 2:1-24; 6:22-25; 2Samuel 24:1-25;
Galatians 3:13-14;

TYPES OF CURSES

1. *Inherited or Generational Curses:* These are curses that are not limited to one generation but are capable of affecting future generations. Most of the curses known to man are of this category. Where this type of curse is in operation patterns of afflictions or situations will be evident from generation to generation or amongst a group of people that share a common characteristic such as pedigree or tribe or heritage. Inherited sicknesses such as asthma, cancer, blood conditions, sickle cell anemia, poor eyesight, etc. are some of the examples of this curse. In this case the demons that enforce the curse had permanently affected the physical genes of those afflicted to such an extent that the sickness or disease is transferred without the physical presence of the demon. This curse can be stopped by destroying the power of the curse over the genes and commanding restoration of the genes to their original created state according to the will of God. Gen. 3:15-19; 9:20-25; Ex. 20:5; Deut. 23:2-3;

2. *Predicated Curses:* These are curses that are connected to disobedience. They are based on acts of obedience or disobedience. For instance the fifth commandment says that if you honor your father and mother your days on earth will be long. This means if you do not honor your father and mother your days on earth may be

short. That is to say if you do not honor your father and mother a curse of untimely death comes upon your life. Another example is if you give your tithes and offerings God will rebuke the devourer for your sake. This means if you do not give your tithes and offerings the devourer stays. The curses of Deuteronomy 28 are all predicated curses. Most predicated curses are by God. Deut. 5:9,16; 28:15-68; Josh. 6:26; 1ki. 16:34; Zech. 5:3-4; Mal. 3:8-11;

3. *Self-imposed Curses:* These are negative pronouncements we make over our lives or circumstances often times in ignorance, rebellion, anger or frustration. These pronouncements or declarations allow for demons of limitation, hindrance or abortion, depending on the nature of the pronouncement to operate in our lives. For instance, prior to the deliverance of Sister Juliet she miscarried and lost all her pregnancies. The reason being that sister Juliet was so pretty she was in love with her figure. So whenever she was pregnant and her figure began to be ruined she would lament and regret the pregnancy and this would trigger the miscarriage. The situation continued until sister Jane was delivered of the spirit of self-obsession amongst others. That is why Proverbs 18:21 declares: *"The tongue has the power of life and death,..."* Our words have over ourselves the same potency that it has over others that we curse. However in the case of

others Proverbs 26:2 declares; **'Like a fluttering sparrow or a darting swallow, an undeserved curse does not come to rest'.** Job 22:28; Jer. 1:9-10; Is. 6:5-7; James 3:1-12;

4. *Vertical Curses;* These refer to curses imposed by those who exercise spiritual authority over us such as our parents, pastors, spouses, leaders, etc. Gen. 9:20-25; 49:3-7;

5. *Horizontal Curses:* These are curses made by our peers or persons not necessarily in authority over us. For this curse to be effective an offense must be involved and the name or authority of a higher spiritual being invoked by the person pronouncing the curse. Num. 22:1-24:25; Pro. 26:2;

HOW TO BREAK A CURSE

1. Confess and Repent of the sin or offense that brought about the curse in the first place. Even if they are the sins of your ancestors that are long gone.

2. Break the curse and all covenants arising from the curse. Sometimes you may need the help of someone with a higher spiritual authority and anointing to effectively break and destroy the power of a curse over you.

3. Bind and cast out of your life permanently the spirits associated with that curse or responsible for enforcing that curse. If it is an inherited sickness then also break the power of that curse

over your genes and command the power of
God to correct every genetic anomaly brought
about by the curse.

4. Destroy the effects or symptoms of the curse
   over your life and command a restoration or
   release of your blessings hindered or tied down
   by the curse.

COVENANTS

Covenants are the most binding and powerful types
of agreements ever made. They are agreements made
consciously or unconsciously by two or more parties
backed by blood sacrifice or the name or authority of a
higher spirit being. Someone could make covenants on
behalf of others that they are in authority over or that
they have a spiritual relationship with. Where
covenants are backed by blood sacrifice it means they
can only be broken by death. In other words those in
covenant would rather die than breach the terms of the
covenant. The terms of the covenant must be observed
even if it means death.

God operates by covenants. He leads people
through covenants because covenants grant Him the
legal access into our lives. Covenants have terms and
penalties. They confer certain rights and demand
certain duties or responsibilities, which attract
penalties if breached. At creation God related with
Adam on the basis of covenant promises. That
covenant gave Adam title to the earth, the Garden of
Eden and God's fellowship but demanded Adams

obedience with respect to the tree of the Knowledge of good and evil. Noah's covenant ensured his protection from flood if he would build an ark according to God's instruction and enter it. Abraham's covenant gave him title to Canaan and the promise of greatness for him and his generations if he would leave his father's house in faith and obey God. This covenant was renewed with Israel through Moses and then expanded to include the gentiles through Christ, itself a fulfillment of the covenant. Today we are enjoying the benefits of the Abrahamic covenant because we have been adopted as sons of Abraham through the blood of Jesus Christ shed on the cross of calvary. Hear Gal. 3:29; '*If you belong to Christ, then you are Abraham's seed, and heirs according to the promise.*

The devil also, the master copycat operates by covenants. Through obedience Adam entered into a covenant of bondage with the devil and relinquished his title to the earth, the Garden of Eden and God's fellowship. That covenant gave the devil legal access into the life of man. Though Christ destroyed the power of this covenant on the cross of Calvary yet it is still in force in the lives of those that have not received Him. And for those that have received Christ the provisions of the annulment of the covenant ought to be enforced through deliverance. The devil is a rebel. He does not respect the law, he only respects power and authority. He does not simply go away just because the power of his covenant of bondage has been destroyed. He must be forced out. In the same way that the provisions of the Abrahamic covenant does not automatically manifest in our lives because we received Christ but has to be possessed through violence, so also the provisions of the covenant of bondage do not automatically disappear with the born again experience, but had to be forced out through deliverance. This is why Obadiah 17, said

> *'But on Mount Zion there shall be deliverance,*
> *And there shall be holiness;*
> *The house of Jacob shall possess their possessions.*

Jesus also declared in Matthew 11:12

> *'And from the days of John the Baptist until now the kingdom of heaven suffers violence, and the violent take it by force.*

Remember also that the Old Testament church had to possess Canaan, their God given inheritance through violence and drove out the inhabitants (a type of demons) by force. In fact they ran into trouble because they did not totally drive out all the inhabitants of Canaan but made treaties and cohabited with some of them. So these demons (inhabitants) became thorns in their flesh and harassed them into sin and rebellion. This is what the church is doing today: cohabiting with demons. That is why the church is still struggling with holiness and with maintaining her victory. The same experience Israel, the Old Testament church had. In Exodus 23:31-33, God set the boundaries of their inheritance and instructed Israel to drive out all the inhabitants of the land;

53

'And I will set your bounds from the Red Sea to the sea, Philistia, and from the desert to the River. For I will deliver the inhabitants of the land into your hand, and you shall drive them out before you. You shall make no covenant with them, nor with their gods. They shall not dwell in your land, lest they make you sin against Me. For if you serve their gods, it will surely be a snare to you."

In Numbers 33:55, God explained the consequences of not totally driving out the inhabitants of the land;

'But if you do not drive out the inhabitants of the land from before you, then it shall be that those whom you let remain shall be irritants in your eyes and thorns in your sides, and they shall harass you in the land where you dwell.

Joshua 13:13, documents the failure of Israel to completely drive out the inhabitants of the land;

'Nevertheless the children of Israel did not drive out the Geshurites or the Maachathites, but the Geshurites and the Maachathites dwell among the Israelites until this day.

Joshua 16:10, further documents that failure;

'And they did not drive out the Canaanites who dwelt in Gezer; but the Canaanites dwell among the

Ephraimites to this day and have become forced laborers.

Joshua 17:12-13, again documents that failure;

'Yet the children of Manasseh could not drive out the inhabitants of those cities, but the Canaanites were determined to dwell in that land. And it happened, when the children of Israel grew strong, that they put the Canaanites to forced labor, but did not utterly drive them out.

The failure of Israel to completely drive out the inhabitants of Canaan (a type of deliverance) is perhaps the most powerful cause of their failure as a nation to walk righteously and maintain the inheritance that God had given them.

Israel, the old testament church is a foreshadow of the new testament church, which instead of driving out the demons within her that are compromising her holiness and victory has entered into alliances with them, justifying them as weaknesses of the flesh and moral failures, common flues that can be cured by a simple repentance. No wonder adultery and divorce and all kinds of demonic manifestations are attaining record levels in the church, more especially in the pulpit.

VERONICA

As we inherit covenants of blessings through Abraham so we inherit covenants of bondage through our ancestry. When our forbears who may have been idol worshippers or members of a religious cult such as freemasonry or Rosicrucianism, bow before an idol, make sacrifices or pray to that false god for the protection of their families, they had knowingly or unknowingly entered in to a covenant binding on every child born or even adopted into that bloodline from generation to generation. This covenant empowers the idol or demonic power behind that idol to inhabit the bodies of all those born into that bloodline perpetually. If for protection, they send demonic 'bodyguards' into the lives of all those born into that family name. This is how many of us were born with strange spirits and strange covenants hovering over our lives. And as we grow up these strange spirits try to establish themselves by causing us to do things (such as demonic incisions, tattoos, visit to witch doctors, or abortion etc.) that would further entrench their positions and attract other demonic forces to live within us. For instance, Veronica was an only child born after a desperate seven year search for children by her parents which took them to every witch doctor and shrine in town, although they were ardent church members. A few years after her birth Veronica was attacked by a nameless illness which medical science had no cure or treatment for. The parents began the rounds of witch doctors and shrines again and after many sacrifices, rituals and demonic incisions Veronica's life was spared. This was Veronica's actual initiation ceremony unknown to her. At 12 Veronica lost her virginity to a 14-year-old boy who collected the blood from the process as a souvenir which it was later revealed he threw into the sea. A further establishment of the covenant. The 14 year old boy died a year later but never ceased to appear in Veronica's dream to have sex with her until she was delivered at age 52. Before her deliverance Veronica's life was scattered. Brilliant, intelligent and beautiful but she never amounted to anything good. She moved with the high and mighty but it never rubbed off. She was low and miserable and could not keep anything intact. She drifted from one affair to the other and even when she got married could not remain faithful to her husband. Her promiscuity and infidelity was legendary. Her health was terrible. She was on the verge of suicide and divorce when the Lord delivered her.

Some of our forbears or us were born out of a specific request for children made to demons, idols, shrines, rivers, rocks, trees etc. by our families. This brings us and our entire bloodline into covenant with the demons associated with those idols, rocks or shrines and introduces the spirits of miscarriage, barrenness, death, poverty, spiritual spouse, etc. into our families. For instance, during the deliverance of a lady I will call Jane, the unclean spirit claimed he was living in her womb because Jane's mother had requested for a child from him. According to the spirit, he was to make sure Jane never gives birth in keeping with the terms of the covenant. Jane had been experiencing miscarriages when she came to us. I am sure Jane's mother never intended this. She was only desperate for a child and failed to read the fine print of the covenant she entered while requesting for Jane from the marine spirit. Jane usually felt the presence of the demon as intense heat in her womb during ovulation and pregnancy. Jane has since been delivered of that spirit and now has a baby girl.

Covenants can be entered into through:

1. Sex: in the dream or physical.
2. Eating in the dream or physical.
3. Any form of written or verbal demonic declarations or agreements
4. Participation in demonic rituals, dances, initiations, handshakes or possessing demonic tokens, emblems, artworks, books or property.
5. Obedience to the devil.

UNHOLY SOUL-TIES

'Now when he had finished speaking to Saul, the soul of Jonathan was knit to the soul of David, and Jonathan loved him as his own soul.' 1 Samuel 18:1

An unholy soul-tie is the spiritual knitting of the souls of two persons to the magnitude that it allows the spirit operating in one person to access the life of the other for the purpose of controlling the behavior and destiny of that person. From the above quoted scripture it is evident that there are holy or positive soul-ties. Positive soul ties like that of a mother and her child or between a teacher and student, or a mentor and protégée are essential for mentoring and spiritual support systems. They enhance communication, understanding and empathy. For instance it is almost impossible to effectively pastor a congregation without a positive soul-tie between pastor and members. In the same way a mother cannot lovingly and effectively cater for her children without a form of soul-tie with them. Nevertheless whenever a soul-tie positive or negative creates an unhealthy element of control directly or by subtlety, controlling manipulating and witchcraft spirits come into play. It does not matter if that soul-tie is with your parents, siblings or your spouse, it is unholy. Oftentimes soul-ties which began positively are exploited by the dominant party for selfish motives, to express their individual desire, dream, character or destiny at the expense of the unique purpose, dream and vision for which the other party was created by God. Thus the weaker party loses their unique identity and reflects the identity, opinion and dream of the dominant party. This is common in relationships between parents and children, pastors and members, mentors and protégées and even spouses. We must be careful of any soul-tie that is dominating or controlling whether directly or by manipulation. Where the spirit of the Lord is there is liberty. We should lead and guide rather than be bossy and controlling. We could end up allowing strange spirits of control, intimidation, provocation, pride, low self esteem, rejection, envy, bitterness, etc. into our lives.

HOW DO WE ENTER INTO SOUL TIES

1. *Sex:* Whenever you engage in a sexual act with someone, you have entered into a soul tie with that person. According to 1 Corinthians 6:16, *'..he who is joined to a harlot is one body with her..'* This is why I believe God is so angry at fornication and adultery in the scriptures. It is a violation of an individuals spiritual space and security. One of the reasons why some born again persons who had led promiscuous lives before their salvation have been unable to find a life partner is because they have not broken the soul-ties resulting from their many sexual acts. Although they are no longer in those relationships in the natural yet in the realm of the spirit they are not single. They are married. Hence no one will marry an already married person. Similarly many marriages are unstable because the parties come into the relationship with unbroken soul-ties. There personalities of past relationships manifesting in the marriage. In the realm of the spirit the marriage appears as a polygamous/polyandrous relationship. Consequently there is chaos.

2. *Ridiculous Love/friendship Covenants:* Some of us in our youthful past had entered into love or friendship covenants with others by mixing our blood or saliva to drink or engaging in rituals of devotion and commitment contrary to the word of God. These blood covenants create unholy soul-ties. For example the case of

Gloria and Greg. As teenagers Gloria and Greg were in love and vowed to spend the rest of their lives together. To demonstrate the seriousness of their vows they cut their thumbs and squeezed blood into the hole of a padlock, locked the padlock and threw both the padlock and the key into the river. A few years later, Gloria's parents moved to another city and Gloria never saw Greg again. At first it was very difficult for Gloria to get married. But after numerous prayers, several broken engagements and almost at the cost of her life she finally married Tony. Then having children became a problem. Gloria could not get pregnant, several surgeries and invitro-fertilizations notwithstanding. These along with other pressures made the marriage so unstable that at the time we met Gloria she was heading for the divorce courts. Through deliverance and the gift of word of knowledge this unholy soul-tie was discovered to be at the root of all Gloria's problems. Once this was taken care of Gloria's marriage was restored and she had since had her third child.

3. *Naming children after dead relatives or idols:* Children named after dead relatives tend to have soul-ties with the ghosts of those dead relatives. The practice of naming Children after dead relatives appears to be predicated on the doctrine of re-incarnation, which is contrary to the word of God. Those that name their children after dead relatives tend to see in the

child the image, personality and spirit of the dead relative. In fact most of them believe the child is the dead relative that has returned. Nowhere in the scriptures were children named after dead relatives. They were usually named after Jehovah's many attributes and miracles. Whenever we name children after dead relatives we open them up for invasion by the spirits of the dead usually demons. Similarly whenever we name children after an idol or a deity or in honor of that deity or idol a soul-tie is created that allows that demon spirit to operate in the life of that child.

Split Personalities:

There are soul-ties in the spiritual realm that appears to confuse the identity and personality of those involved. Cases of conflicting or split personalities are manifestations of demonic soul-ties. For instance a lady I will call Beatrice had an uncanny habit of manifesting oftentimes opposing extremes of behavior and ability in the natural that makes her very unpredictable and impossible. Though her name was Beatrice in the natural yet she found herself being addressed as Princess Jemina in her dreams. During her deliverance, a demon claiming to be her spiritual father threatened to take Beatrice with him if forced to leave. Initially we ignored the threats and Beatrice almost passed away. However on the leading of the Holy Ghost we asked the demon spirit what the name of his daughter was. He said 'Princess Jemina'. When we insisted that the lady's name was not Princess Jemina but Beatrice, he disagreed vehemently. Then we applied Hebrews 4:12 to severe the soul-tie between Beatrice and Princess Jemina and the demon spirit left without threatening the life of Beatrice. Princess Jemina was the split personality of Beatrice.

YOKES, SPELLS AND ENCHANTMENTS

These are demonic webs, clouds or weights cast over the lives or destinies of persons through powerful pronouncements and incantations. They allow demons of limitations, disfavor and spiritual parasites to cleave to people like leaches, hang around them, cast shadows on their lives and try to hinder the blessings of God in the life of the victims. These demons do not necessarily reside in the body of the victim. They usually stay within his or her spiritual space (as strongmen; Matthew 12:29) and place a lid over the entrance of blessings or act as leakage for spiritual strength and vitality. Some of them simply divert the blessings or scare away any person through whom the blessing may come. Naomi had a spell cast over her life by her stepmother, which she did not know about. However she observed that best friends will suddenly hate her for no apparent reason. Employers and bosses will suddenly dislike her without explanation. She carries an aura that once she gets into a place or amongst people they just hate her without even knowing why. In relationships whenever any body indicates any interest in marrying Naomi, they will suddenly perceive a foul body odor that repels them.

No one including Naomi perceives this foul odor. And those that perceive it, do so only after they have considered getting more serious with Naomi. Consequently she had a high turnover of jobs, friends and engagements until she was delivered and that spell broken over her.

Involvement with palmistry, fortune telling, divination, horoscope, Ouiija board and the like, even as a joke, usually opens the door for a spiritual weight, web or negative clouds to be placed over our lives.

Incisions and tattoos:

'Do not cut your bodies for the dead or put tattoo marks on yourselves. I am the LORD.' Lev. 19:28

Any permanent marking on the flesh that is not due to accident or medical surgery, constitutes a transgression of the above command. Incisions are covenant markings of ownership or rights upon the lives of the people by the demon spirits in honor of whom these markings were done. People are always deceived into believing that these markings are done just to heal one sickness or the other. They are not. Even tribal marks represent tribal covenants to tribal deities, interwoven with cultural practices. Similarly tattoos done in honor of a person, in a love relationship, an idea, or as a fad usually creates a soul-tie with that person or animal or the spirit behind that idea and opens the door for those spirits or other related spirits of lawlessness to invade our spiritual space. The scriptures reveal that in the last days people will be compelled to take the mark of the beast on their foreheads or their hands as a gesture of worship and allegiance to the anti-christ. The scripture also reveals that whoever accepts the mark of the beast is condemned already irrespective of what they do. If that is the case then wearing a tattoo or permanent marks of any kind is not as harmless as the world is trying to make it seem. Revelation 13:16-17; 14:9-11; 20:4

HOW DO I KNOW THAT I AM DEMONIZED

1. *BY DISCERNMENT:* Discernment is a gift of the Holy Ghost that sensitizes one to the operation of spirits. By the operation of this gift you or a deliverance minister could determine if you are demonized and the kind of spirits in operation.

2. *BY DREAMS AND VISIONS:* These are some of the most common ways through which we can tell if we are demonized or not. Although we are not ruled by dreams, dreams give us an indication of what may be going on in our spiritual environment. Numbers 12:6 tells us that God speaks to us through dreams and visions. Job 33:14-18 confirms this. Long before I was delivered I had this reoccurring dream of having sex with a woman but I did not understand it. She would come with different faces, sometimes taking on the faces of women that are familiar to me and those I lusted after. Still I dismissed it as mere dreams

or products of the flesh, until a man of God discerned that I was demonized. Offended I prayed desperately for a revelation from God to disprove the man of God and that night the woman appeared in my dreams claiming to by my spiritual wife. Angry I lunched into a 6-day marathon fast seeking deliverance and opened up a can of worms. God opened my eyes to a shocking revelation of the number and type of demons that were crawling under my skin. As I got rid of one set of demons another set revealed themselves. It was as if they were in layers upon layers concealed by ignorance and my sanctimonious, Pentecostal, tongue talking, self-righteousness and spirituality. A holy rage welled up inside of me and that is how I got into the deliverance ministry.

3. *BY OBSERVATION (SYMPTOMATICALLY):* How does a doctor diagnose an ailment? By observing the symptoms. What are the symptoms produced by your life? What are the patterns or cycles observed in your life, relationship, finances etc.? Do they suggest a predominance of demonic activity? Similarly you may not know if there are mice and roaches in your house until you observe their destructive acts. What destructive act is the devil carrying out in your life? Are you always sick? There could be a spirit of infirmity operating in your life. Are you always broke? A spirit of lack or poverty could be responsible. Is your marriage unstable, have you been

divorced many times, do you find it difficult to keep a relationship going or are you barren? These are symptoms of the presence of a spiritual spouse. By observing the symptoms of your life you can tell if you are demonized or not.

4. *BY DEDUCTION:* John 8:34 says that whoever commits sin is a slave of sin. So if you lie always, you are demonized by a lying spirit. If you commit adultery you are demonized by a spirit of adultery. If you were dedicated to an idol you do not need any one to tell you that the demon spirit behind that idol may be indwelling you. If your parents were members of the occult, then you could be demonized by occult spirits. By simple deduction we may come to understand that there could be contrary spirits operating in certain areas of our lives.

TREATMENT

Mark 16:17
And these signs will follow those who believe: In My name they will cast out demons;

Luke 9:1
Then He called His twelve disciples together and gave them power and authority over all demons, and to cure diseases.

Luke 10:17
Then the seventy returned with joy, saying, "Lord, even the demons are subject to us in Your name.

Luke 10:19
Behold, I give you the authority to trample on serpents and scorpions, and over all the power of the enemy, and nothing shall by any means hurt you.

TYPES OF DELIVERANCE

The actual casting out of demons is strictly a Holy Ghost affair through the vessel that is being used. Knowledge of the word, holy lifestyle, baptism of the Holy Ghost and operation of the gifts of the spirit on the part of the minister are essential for best results without devastating counter attacks. The prayer process through which the recipient should be led includes:

1. Repentance for own sin and sins of fathers, ancestry, pedigree, tribe etc. as the case may be.
2. Verbal and vocal renunciation and breaking of covenants, curses, yokes, spells, enchantments etc. Where soul-ties are involved they must be severed also and the demons associated with the soul-ties cast out.
3. Binding the demons and casting them out of your body and your life. As well as forbidding them to return.
4. Commanding all demonic properties and strongholds to be dismantled, destroyed and consumed by the fire of the Holy Ghost.
5. Releasing and restoring back all that the devil had stolen or destroyed through bondage.

There are three types of deliverance as follows:

Self Deliverance:

There are some spirits that you can cast out of yourself without the help of a deliverance minister. But there are others that may require a higher anointing to deal with. Nevertheless every believer should be able to carry out some level of self-deliverance or it would be difficult to maintain the deliverance. You may not be able to cast out demons out of others until you have enough faith to cast them out of yourself. And you are ordained to cast out demons.

Process Deliverance:

Deliverance is a process that could take an hour, several hours, a whole day, weeks or even months. This is because even if the demons leave immediately they are commanded to leave, most of the time they return to demonized that person again perhaps because the habits associated with that spirit was not broken or because the spirit man of that person is not strong enough to resist the onslaught of the demons. Other times the toughness of the demon, the insufficiency of the faith of the minister, the unwillingness of the patient or their emotional and spiritual immaturity can lengthen the battle to expel the demons. Catherine, a sixteen year old girl had been covenanted to a very stubborn demon from her mothers womb. Whenever we cast this demon out and he leaves Catherine will loose her mind and unable to function normally. This continued repeatedly until the spirit of the Lord revealed unto us that Catherine's emotional and mental superstructure was so dependent on that demon that when he leaves she's messed up. On the direction of the Holy Ghost we locked the demon in a box inside Catherine and forbade him to operate until she was emotionally and mentally matured enough to be delivered and that was two years later. It is also interesting to note that Catherine was unreceptive and hostile to the word of God until that spirit was locked up in her.

Instantaneous and Distance Deliverance:

I used to teach that deliverance must be process until I went back to the scriptures and discovered that

Jesus had a lot of instantaneous deliverance. I began to exercise my faith in that direction and God confirmed his word. It is possible to be delivered instantly. Some people are delivered instantly at the point of salvation. I have had dozens of cases where the demon spirits left immediately and returned no more. Similarly I thought that for deliverance to take place the patient must be physically present. But God has shown through practical experience and the scriptures that deliverance can take place by the prophetic word being spoken over vast distances and without anyone laying hands on the patient. Acts 19:12 stated that aprons and handkerchiefs taken from the body of Apostle Paul when used on those oppressed of the devil brought about deliverance instantly. Today I conduct major deliverances over the telephone and the demons do manifest and leave for good. Sharon called me (in Houston) from Delaware. She had had four broken engagements and was on the verge of suicide. I conducted deliverance for her over the phone and she manifested and vomited in her home in Delaware. She got delivered and baptized in the Holy Ghost. Eight months later she was married.

How Demons Leave:

Demons are spirits without bodies as such they are like breath or air. They usually leave through tears, yawning, sweating, gassing, vomiting, running nose, excretion, urination, menstrual circle and discharges. Some leave immediately, others over a period of time. Demons do not have to manifest in order to leave. Some leave without manifesting. Some even leave without prayer, once the recipient walks into the anointed atmosphere.

DEALING WITH DEMONIC PROPERTIES OR DEPOSITS:

Just like we move into a house with all kinds of furniture and properties even so demons move into people with all kinds of junk furniture and properties. These properties along with the habits that they initiate constitute the strongholds of these demons. According to Matthew 12:43-45

When an unclean spirit goes out of a man, he goes through dry places, seeking rest, and finds none. **44 Then he says, 'I will return to my house from which I came.' And when he comes, he finds it empty, swept, and put in order.** *45 Then he goes and takes with him seven other spirits more wicked than himself, and they enter and dwell there; and the last state of that man is worse than the first. So shall it also be with this wicked generation."*

Verse 44 says when the unclean spirit returns he finds it empty, swept and put in order. This means while the unclean spirit was there the house or body was filled, (with junk properties) dirty and in disorder. Or else why will it be swept? If what was there was good property why sweep it out? In fact I believe the reason the unclean spirit goes to invite seven more spirits more wicked than himself is to put up a defense because he just discovered that his strongholds (furniture, properties and habits) had been dismantled and removed. And those were his defenses. During deliverance sessions I see these properties with the eye of the spirit as nails, pins, teeth, bones, stones, belts, chains, calabashes, animals & birds, fish scales, dead meat, eggs, cowries, beads, extra eyes, thrones, crowns, ornaments, ropes, filthy garments, growths, debris etc. There are also those properties such as buildings, cars, thrones, offices, titles, spiritual children etc. that may not be in the body of the patient but that are allocated to the patient in the demonic world. All these have to be renounced, consumed and destroyed by the fire of the Holy Ghost. If not destroyed, these properties or deposits make the deliverance more difficult, weaken the ability of the patient to resist re-entry by that demon and serve as a magnet to attract the demon back.

The Role of Fasting:

Deliverance can take place with out fasting on the part of the patient but it may not be maintained with out it. This is because fasting is a requirement for the Christian walk, for consecration, sanctification, building up the spirit man, energizing the faith, adding fervency to prayer and crucifying the flesh. Paul said in 1st Corinthians 9:27 that he keeps his body under and brings it into subjection; how? I believe through fasting and prayer. In fact according to Matthew 17:21, prayer and fasting is a cure for unbelief. Faith comes by hearing the word of God but it is energized,

sustained and activated by prayer and fasting. See the
story in Matthew 17:14-21

*14 And when they had come to the multitude, a
man came to Him, kneeling down to Him and saying,
15 "Lord, have mercy on my son, for he is an
epileptic and suffers severely; for he often falls into
the fire and often into the water. 16 So I brought him
to Your disciples, but they could not cure him." 17
Then Jesus answered and said, "O faithless and
perverse generation, how long shall I be with you?
How long shall I bear with you? Bring him here to
Me." 18 And Jesus rebuked the demon, and it came
out of him; and the child was cured from that very
hour. 19 Then the disciples came to Jesus privately
and said, "Why could we not cast him out?" 20 So
Jesus said to them, "Because of your unbelief; for
assuredly, I say to you, if you have faith as a mustard
seed, you will say to this mountain, 'Move from here
to there,' and it will move; and nothing will be
impossible for you. 21 However, this kind does not go
out except by prayer and fasting."*

In my experience fasting on the part of the patient
is essential for the following reasons;

1. It energizes the faith.
2. It weakens the flesh and breaks its resistance to
   deliverance, making the patient more
   submissive to the deliverance process.
3. By weakening the flesh it destroys the base on
   which the strongholds and deposits were built

and in the process makes the destruction of demonic properties, deposits and strongholds easier.

4. Along with the word of God it strengthens the spirit man against the return of the demon spirit.

Similarly fasting on the part of the minister that is ministering the deliverance not necessarily at the point of ministration cannot be overemphasized. I believe a deliverance minister should live a fasting lifestyle in order to, amongst other reasons, enhance their sensitivity to the spirit and build up spiritual immunity to counter attacks.

How do I know that I am delivered?

1. *By faith:* Mark 11:24 says, **'Therefore I say to you, whatever things you ask when you pray, believe that you receive them, and you will have them.** And John 8:36 guarantees, **'Therefore if the Son makes you free, you shall be free indeed.**

2. *By revelation:* God could show you in a dream, vision, word of Knowledge, prophetic word, discernment or by the inner witness of the Holy Spirit your deliverance and victory.

3. *By observation of symptoms:* When you are delivered you will experience change. The symptoms you used to see will not be there anymore. But you must also understand that the virus may be dead long before the symptoms

completely varnish. And that you may need to apply other medications for complete restoration. For instance if you had been oppressed by a demon of hindrance and poverty. After deliverance you may still be poor if you do not tithe and give. It is no more the demon that is hindering you now but yourself.

Seven things that hinder deliverance:

1. *Sin.*
2. *unbelief*
3. *unforgiveness/bitterness*
4. *unwillingness*
5. *self consciousness*
6. *pride*
7. *self righteousness*

BATTLE IN THE HEAVENLIES

(*The story of Iyabo's deliverance*)

By the time we met her, Iyabo had come to the end of the road. Her life was miserable, her marriage unstable, her finances destroyed and her peace stolen. All these were not necessarily her making. She was initiated to be the priestess of some of the most powerful deities in both the Bini and Yoruba kingdoms in Nigeria, by her grandparents. But she wanted no part of it. So she opted for Jesus in 1993 and her problems intensified. In her quest for solution she went from city to city, church to church and pastor to pastor all to no avail. But God had timing and a plan. We placed her on twenty-one days of marathon fasting and prayer, which coincided, with the church's annual forty-day fast. Only ministers who had been in several days of fasting participated in the deliverance prayers for Iyabo, which took place daily. After fifteen days the demons were yet to be moved but we were undaunted. On the final day we gathered again around Iyabo, binding, loosing, violent in the spirit and tonguing. The air was thick with prayer and laden with the anointing yet the demons resisted. Obviously there was war in the heavenlies but to all appearances the war was heading to a stalemate. The Holy Ghost prompted, its time to change the battle strategy. We lifted up the banner of praise and the glory of the Lord came down. The hornet stirred. Iyabo dazed two lightning steps back, sprang up and got into intensive dancing, lurid eyeballs closed amidst stupefied laughter. Praise and Hallelujah stunned the air. The Lord reigneth, let the earth tremble. Suddenly Iyabo stopped, stamped her feet, shook her head in anger and with a loud and bitter voice the spirits cried, Noooooo! Noooooo! Noooooo! How can? Impossible! A fierce exchange ensued between the spirits in Iyabo and the deliverance ministers. Below are excerpts.

Demon spirit:
   Leave us alone! What is your own?

David Okumgba

Minister:
Who are you?

Demon spirit:
Leave us alone. Ah! Ah! Ah! Ah!

Minister:
What is your name?...Pause...(PRAISE SINGING RESUMES)

Demon spirit:
Aquar! Aquar!

Minister:
How many are you?

Demon spirit:
We are many...(REFUSES TO SPEAK FURTHER) PRAISE SINGING AGAIN... DEMONS TORMENTED...

Minister:
What are you doing here? Get out in Jesus name!!!

Demon spirit:
She was given to us. Her grandmother gave her to us before she was born. Her mother did not know we had an agreement.

Minister:
Well, this daughter of Abraham has been bought with the blood of Jesus and that nullifies your

agreement. She has given her life to Jesus and that cancels your covenant.

Demon spirit:

She belongs to us. We did not beg or ask for her. Her grandmother gave her to us. We know the rules, we stayed in our kingdom and she came to us. What mark of ownership do you have? Have you seen her head, waist, legs, hand, tongue, and ear? Our mark is upon her. Even on her chest and her back. Check she is ours.

Minister:

I do not go by what I see. I go by the word of God. The blood of Jesus is upon her and that is our mark of ownership. I stand upon the authority of the church and I command you to release her in Jesus name.

Demon spirit:

No! No! We do not doubt that. But we have our rights and there are rules. We did not ask for her. The covenant is that she cannot have children. All her children are for us. We stand on our rights.

Minister:

He who breaks the edge the serpent will bite. You have transgressed the law because this daughter is the anointed of the Lord and you have chosen to torment her. It is written 'touch not my anointed and do my prophets no harm'. He whom the Lord shall set free is free indeed. The Lord Jesus Christ has paid the price for her and that you cannot challenge. He has set her

David Okumgba

free so you cannot hold her bound. The blood of Jesus is stronger than any other covenant or blood covenant and it has erased all your marks and claims over her life. So take all your properties and leave in Jesus name!

Demon spirit:
She will pay for it oh! She will pay. Once we catch her that is the end. She belonged to us before she decided to go over to the other side. She dared to burn all our properties and shrines in public and disgrace us. She will pay for it. You have been shielding her. Every time you people cover her. Which child does she want? She runs from pillar to post. We won't agree o! if she wants a child she should take it from us. If you give her a child we will take it. We will take it!

Minister:
Aquar! Pack your load and go in Jesus name! What do you have in this body?

Demon spirit:
…(CRYING BITTERLY)… She is a silly girl. She refused to wear the crown. She is always cutting her hair. Her legs belong to us. That is where we play.

Minister:
I soak the legs in the bloooooood of Jeeesus!

Demon spirit:
…SCREAMS…LEGS SHAKING VIOLENTLY… TREMBLING ALLOVER… GYRATES…

Minister:
Aquar! Take all your property and go in Jesus name!

Demon spirit:
Her hips, do you see such around?

Minister:
Take your properties and go!

Demon spirit:
But why me, **'Imose'** (ANOTHER DEMON SPIRIT) is there. She has my properties under her armpits also.

Minister:
Aquar get out of this body in Jesus name!!!...AQUAR CRIED AND LEFT.
...Who is the doorkeeper? Identify yourself.

Demon spirit:
My name is 'Owaifo'.

Minister:
What are you still doing there when your master Aquar has gone? Get out in Jesus name!!!... OWAIFO ROARED AND LEFT...
(MINISTER CALLS)...Imose! Imose!

David Okumgba

Demon spirit:
I am Imose, the beautiful one. Why are you chasing all of us away? Where do you want us to go? We have been here for long.

Minister:
Where did you live before this body came along? Pack your load and go in Jesus name!!!...IMOSE LEAVES IN A WAVE OF MANIFESTATIONS..
Next? Come out in Jesus name!

Demon spirit:
I am the prince of Bini kingdom. I look after my domain.

Minister:
Well, you are a bold one. But listen, the Prince of Peace is Jesus. Great is the Lord. The Lord of the whole earth. I come in his name. The name of Jesus that has been exalted above all principalities and governments. So take all your properties and go in Jesus name!!!

Demon spirit:
I will leave but let me take my bead on her forehead...ROARS... HEAD VIBRATING AND LEAVES.

Minister:
Next? Come out in your order and leave.

Demon spirit:

I am 'Augu'...MANIFESTS SELF PITY AND LEAVES...

Demon spirit:

I am 'Sango'. She used to dance for me. She performed my rites to the end. She is mine. Did you not see her dance?...ROARS AND LEAVES...

Demon spirit:

I am 'Ayah'...(MAKING HEAT MOTIONS)... I am the fire she used to see. I came when she was eight years old but I will leave now... LEAVES...

Demon spirit:

I am 'Ifa'. She is my priestess!

Minister:

What! The Lord is indignant against you. There can be no enchantment against Judah nor is there any divination against Israel. Get out in Jesus name! How did you return?

Demon spirit:

Her grandfather was my priest. She performed my rites to the second stage. She is mine! But don't torment me. Let me go. I will take my ax which I threw at her head at the last deliverance in Kaduna (NIGERIA) because she wanted to leave me. I gave her blinding headache. I am leaving now... LEAVES..

David Okumgba

Minister:
Who is that large yellow woman at her back? What are you doing there?

Demon spirit:
...LAUGHS... So you saw me. I am 'Aiyeke'. I stay at her back, that is my name. I am assigned to follow her anywhere she goes. I am responsible for covering the pregnancies so no medical machine can see it. They see me instead. I sit on the pregnancy and push it down. It must not stay.

Minister:
You are the one I have been looking for. You caused the mysterious disappearance of pregnancies. You manipulate it and push it down. Now the church rebukes you in the name of Jesus Christ and we terminate all your activities. Get out in Jesus name!!!...AIYEKE LEAVES WITH A LOUD SHRIEK...

Demon spirit:
...SHAKING OF LEGS... LIMPING AND GROANING...

Minister:
What is that? Who are you?

Demon spirit:
We attacked her left knee. We were sent to cripple it by her aunt when she was eleven years old. We

caused her knee to shift and afflicted her with great pain.

Minister:

Your contract has ended. Pack your load and go in Jesus name!!!... CRIED AND LEFT...

Iyabo is now free. Praise God!

David Okumgba

MANAGEMENT
Maintaining your deliverance

Luke 11:24-26
"When an unclean spirit goes out of a man, he goes through dry places, seeking rest; and finding none, he says, 'I will return to my house from which I came.' And when he comes, he finds it swept and put in order. Then he goes and takes with him seven other spirits more wicked than himself, and they enter and dwell there; and the last state of that man is worse than the first."

WHY DEMONS HOLD ON

Demons do not give up unless compelled by superior power. Demons are rebellious spirits diametrically opposed to the will, counsel and word of God. They cannot be convinced, negotiated, persuaded or cajoled out. They can only be forced out by superior power and wisdom. Besides their rebellious nature demons have a strong incentive for resisting expulsion from their human abode. Below are some of their reasons for holding on.

1. **They can only find rest and peace inside a natural body.** According to the scripture passage quoted above,(Luke 11:24-26) when an unclean spirit goes out of a man, he goes through dry places seeking rest. If he is seeking rest in dry places it

means that he had rest while he was in the body of the victim and his rest is now threatened because he does not have the human shield for a covering any more. This makes me wonder. Could it be that demons outside their human shield are exposed to attacks by the forces of light, since the war between the forces of darkness and the forces of light is a continuos one? Yes or why else would the demons be desperate to return to the house from which they came because they could not find rest anywhere else. This explains why the demons named legion that possessed the man from the Gaderenes of Mark 5:1-16, begged Jesus to permit them to enter the swine. Demons are in danger of being attacked by the forces of light if they are outside a natural body. Warfare prayers prayed by intercessors like guided missiles are hunting demons whenever they are exposed. Therefore if you allow a demon spirit to be comfortable in your body you may be unconsciously aiding a demon spirit to escape the bullets of the forces of light. Then whose side are you really on?

2. **Being inside a body gives them better access and leverage to influence the mind of man.**

1 Corinthians 2:11; says *'For who among men knows the thoughts of a man except the man's spirit within him? In the same way no one knows the thoughts of God except the Spirit of God.*

Inside the body demons are in a better position to learn the thoughts and things of a person and manipulate these to influence the person negatively against God.

3. **Being inside a body gives them better control of that body as a weapon against the soul and spirit of the man.**

Galatians 5:16-17 reveals; '*I say then: Walk in the Spirit, and you shall not fulfill the lust of the flesh. For the flesh lusts against the Spirit, and the Spirit against the flesh; and these are contrary to one another, so that you do not do the things that you wish*

There is a battle for control between the flesh and the spirit in the battleground of the soul. So when demons indwell a body they strengthen the flesh to resist the spirit in the same way the spirit of God comes to strengthen our inner man against the flesh. (Ephesians 3:16). The presence of these demonic spirits oftentimes causes us to do what we do not wish to do. This was Paul's agony in Romans 7:15-25

For what I am doing, I do not understand. For what I will to do, that I do not practice; but what I hate, that I do. 16 If, then, I do what I will not to do, I agree with the law that it is good. 17 But now, it is no longer I who do it, but sin that dwells in me. 18 For I know that in me (that is, in my flesh) nothing good dwells; for to will is present with me, but how to perform what is good I do not find. 19 For the good that I will to do, I do not do; but the evil I will not to do, that I practice. 20 Now if I do what I will not to do, it is no longer I who do it, but sin that dwells in me. 21 I find then a law, that evil is present with me, the one who wills to do good. 22 For I delight in the law of God according to the inward man. 23 But I see another law in my members, warring against the law of my mind, and bringing me into captivity to the law of sin which is in my members. 24 O wretched man that I am! Who will deliver me from this body of death? 25 I thank God—through Jesus Christ our Lord! So then, with the mind I myself serve the law of God, but with the flesh the law of sin.

HOW DO I KEEP DEMONS OUT?

Deliverance will have been a lot easier if demons do not attempt to return back to their abodes after they had been cast out. The fact that they do as Jesus taught in Matthew 12:43-45 and Luke 11:24-26 makes it imperative that we must understand ways of keeping them out when they attempt to return. As with medical ailments we need to manage our physical hygiene, nutrition and exercise to avoid the disease from reoccurring even so we must manage our spiritual hygiene, nutrition and exercise in other to enable us resist any demonic onslaught, invasion or contamination. Here are seven principles for maintaining your deliverance;

Break and resist old negative habits and attitudes:

When demons inhabit a body they build strongholds in the life of that person by acquiring demonic properties or furniture and creating negative habits. For instance a spirit of anger in a man will initiate the habit of anger. The habit of anger becomes the stronghold and defense for the spirit of anger because even if the spirit is cast out the person will still be bound by the habit and that could also provide the legal basis and magnet for the spirit to re-enter the person. Similarly the habits of stinginess and laziness are some of the strongholds of the spirit of poverty. The attitude of impatience is the stronghold of a hasty and proud spirit. And the habit of self-pity or depression is the stronghold of the spirit of rejection. There are also undue attachments to jewelry, cars, clothing, food, money and so on that are initiated by demonic presence that must be broken if deliverance must be maintained successfully. However while demonic properties could be destroyed supernaturally through prayer and fasting, habits and attitudes need the deliberate exercise of the will in obedience to the word of God and renewal of the mind for their destruction. The patient must replace old negative habits and attitudes with positive ones in accordance with the scriptures. Hear Romans 12:1-2;

'I beseech you therefore, brethren, by the mercies of God, that you present your bodies a living sacrifice, holy, acceptable to God, which is your reasonable service. And do not be conformed to this world, but be transformed by the renewing of your mind, that you

90

may prove what is that good and acceptable and perfect will of God.

And Ephesians 4:22-24;

'You were taught, with regard to your former way of life, to put off your old self, which is being corrupted by its deceitful desires; to be made new in the attitude of your minds; and to put on the new self, created to be like God in true righteousness and holiness.

Be filled with the Holy Ghost daily:
To be baptized with the Holy Ghost is to be immersed in the Holy Ghost. However we need to be filled with the Holy Ghost daily. This is because it is possible to be immersed in the Holy Ghost and not be filled. It is like immersing a cocked bottle inside water. Unless the bottle is open it may be immersed in water and still be empty of water. Sadly that is the state of a lot of believers in the church that speak empty, ritualistic and powerless tongues. At the baptism of the Holy Ghost in Acts chapter 2 the disciples were filled also but they needed another in-filling of the Holy Ghost in Acts 4:31 as recorded in the scriptures. ***And when they had prayed, the place where they were assembled together was shaken; and they were all filled with the Holy Spirit, and they spoke the word of God with boldness.***
This means that by Acts chapter 4 the in filling of Acts chapter 2 had been depleted, hence the need for another filling. In the same way we get depleted as we

go about the kingdoms business each day and need to be refilled and refreshed by the Holy Ghost.

Stay under an adequate spiritual cover:

In God's program, man ought to belong to a natural family and a spiritual family. As the natural family provides man with a natural covering and inheritance even so the spiritual family provides man with spiritual covering and inheritance. In other words every believer no matter how spiritual or anointed ought to belong to a church family. This is particularly pertinent if you are going through deliverance. Not only must a deliverance patient belong to a church, they must be committed to that church in every way possible. Whenever they walk in disobedience or rebellion to that church or its authority they loose the cover and are exposed. The devil knows it when the hedge has been removed. It is also important that the church must be one commissioned by God not by man and that is still walking in the light of that commission. A young man that was delivered but was yet to enter into his breakthrough once complained about the incessant harassment of the devil and the spirit of the Lord instructed him through me to go and be a worker in his church. And once he did that, the harassment ceased and he walked into his breakthrough.

Regular spiritual tune-ups:

If our natural self needs regular medical check-ups, our souls also needs regular spiritual check-ups and tune-ups. This is because as we interact each day we get spiritually contaminated through the things we see, hear, think, touch, speak and feel. We ought to submit ourselves periodically to the Holy Ghost and to our mentors for examination and cleansing as the case may be. This kind of tune up may involve periodic seasons of consecration, fasting and praying. ***For if we would judge ourselves, we would not be judged. 1Corinthians 11:31.***

Watch and Pray:

Christians pray they hardly watch. Consequently they walk into the snares of the devil or they do not know when the devil has stolen his way into their lives. To watch is to be alert and sensitive to your spiritual environment. We must watch our dreams, visions, tongue, how we see and hear, our thought life, our work life, our walk life, our attachments, our feelings, our association etc. We must stop taking things for granted and walking presumptuously. Mark 14:38 says, ***Watch and pray, lest you enter into temptation.*** Proverbs 22:3 says, ***A prudent man foresees evil and hides himself...***

Be armed with the word of God:

Rev. 12:11 declares, '***And they overcame him by the blood of the Lamb and by the word of their testimony, and they did not love their lives to the death.*** The word of God is our weapon for overcoming the devil. Jesus used it against every temptation thrown at him at the wilderness. It is the instrument for renewing our minds, for direction and guidance, for healing and deliverance, for guaranteed success, for waging a good warfare, for victorious living and for securing our heritage in Christ Jesus. A believer without the word is like a gun without bullets. The word of God is one of the most potent weapons for keeping demons out of your life. Resist the devil and he will flee from you.

Live a holy lifestyle:

Sin brings in the devil but holiness keeps him out. If you continue in sin after you have been delivered it is only a matter of time before the demons return successfully. For whoever commits sin is a slave of sin. John 8:34.